This book is to be returned on or before
the last date stamped below.

KINGFISHER
An imprint of Larousse plc
Elsley House, 24–30 Great Titchfield Street,
London W1P 7AD

This edition published by Kingfisher 1996
(hb) 10 9 8 7 6 5 4 3 2 1
(pb) 10 9 8 7 6 5 4 3 2 1
Copyright © Larousse plc 1995

Previously published by Kingfisher 1995 in the *Little Library* series

A CIP catalogue record for this book is
available from the British Library.

ISBN 0 7534 0094 4 (hb)
ISBN 0 7534 0095 2 (pb)

Editor: Deri Robins
Author: Christopher Maynard
Glossary: Charlotte Evans
Consultant: Dr Paul Bahn
Cover illustration: Shirley Tourret (BL Kearley)
Illustrators: Angus McBride (Linden Artists) 14–15, 22–23, 28–29;
Peter Bull 6–7, 19, 21, 25, 29; John Haysom 3, 5, 11, 12–13; John
James (Temple Rogers) 10–11, 24; David Salariya 23.

Printed in Hong Kong

LITTLE HISTORIES

Stone Age Times

Christopher Maynard

Kingfisher

Contents

The first humans

About six million years ago, Africa was covered in forest. In time, many forests turned into dry grasslands, and the apes that lived there had to learn new skills in order to survive.

Some apes began to stand upright, so that they could look out over the grass for their enemies. By about 4.5 million years ago, they had turned into the ancestors of humans – the ape-like *Australopithecus*.

The wanderers

F or millions of years, these ape-like ancestors of ours lived only in the African grasslands. Then, nearly two million years ago, people began to wander all over the Earth.

At first, they spread to Europe and Asia. Later, they reached Australia, and finally America.

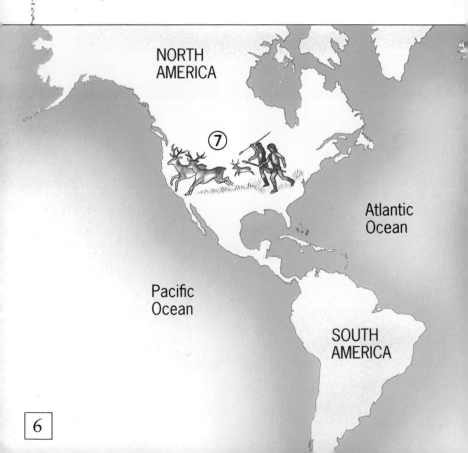

NORTH
AMERICA

⑦

Atlantic
Ocean

Pacific
Ocean

SOUTH
AMERICA

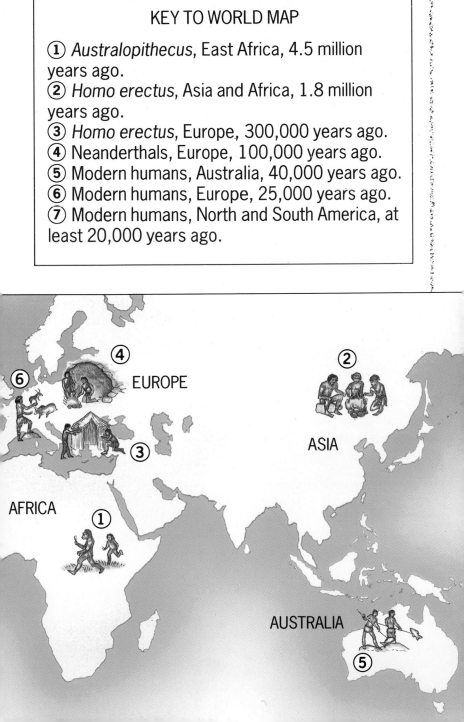

KEY TO WORLD MAP

① *Australopithecus*, East Africa, 4.5 million years ago.
② *Homo erectus*, Asia and Africa, 1.8 million years ago.
③ *Homo erectus*, Europe, 300,000 years ago.
④ Neanderthals, Europe, 100,000 years ago.
⑤ Modern humans, Australia, 40,000 years ago.
⑥ Modern humans, Europe, 25,000 years ago.
⑦ Modern humans, North and South America, at least 20,000 years ago.

EUROPE

ASIA

AFRICA

AUSTRALIA

Faces from the past

W e know what early people looked like because scientists have pieced together the remains of their skulls and teeth. These show how their heads gradually became bigger, and how the long, ape-like jaws of *Homo habilis* (see pages 10–11) grew shorter.

After *Homo habilis* (above) came *Homo erectus* (left). These people had far bigger heads and flatter faces than their ancestors.

The Neanderthals (right) came after *Homo erectus*. From looking at their skulls, scientists have worked out that their brains were the same size as ours – maybe bigger!

THE FIRST PEOPLE

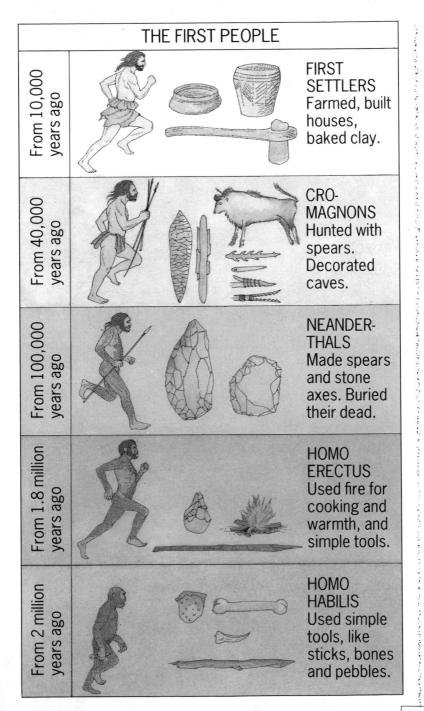

From 10,000 years ago		**FIRST SETTLERS** Farmed, built houses, baked clay.
From 40,000 years ago		**CRO-MAGNONS** Hunted with spears. Decorated caves.
From 100,000 years ago		**NEANDER-THALS** Made spears and stone axes. Buried their dead.
From 1.8 million years ago		**HOMO ERECTUS** Used fire for cooking and warmth, and simple tools.
From 2 million years ago		**HOMO HABILIS** Used simple tools, like sticks, bones and pebbles.

'Handy man'

About two million years ago, the first
real humans appeared. We call
them *Homo habilis*, or 'handy man', as
they were skilled at using simple tools.

Small groups of *Homo habilis*
roamed through eastern Africa, in
grasslands that swarmed with game. If
they came across a good supply of food
and water, they often stopped and built
shelters from stones and branches.

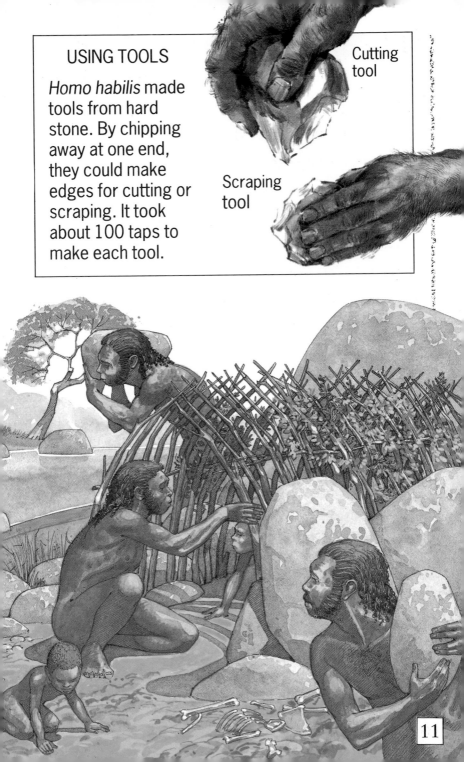

USING TOOLS

Homo habilis made tools from hard stone. By chipping away at one end, they could make edges for cutting or scraping. It took about 100 taps to make each tool.

Cutting tool

Scraping tool

11

'Upright man'

Homo erectus ('upright man') were the next people to appear. Their remains have been found by scientists in many different parts of the world.

These people were skilful hunters, who used wooden spears to catch all kinds of animals. They would drag the bodies back to their camps, where they used stone hand-axes to skin and cut up the meat. They built fires to cook the food, and to give them warmth. Fires also kept wild animals at bay.

'Wise man'

About 100,000 years ago, a new kind of people appeared. We call them *Homo sapiens*, or 'wise man', and know that they lived in Europe during the last Ice Age.

Among these people was a group called the Neanderthals. They were strong, intelligent people, who lived in caves and made warm clothes from animal skins.

CHANGING SKULLS

Like ourselves, the Neanderthals ① were *Homo sapiens*. However, these people had heavier jaws and flatter skulls than we have today.

Modern skull shapes ② only became common 40,000 years ago.

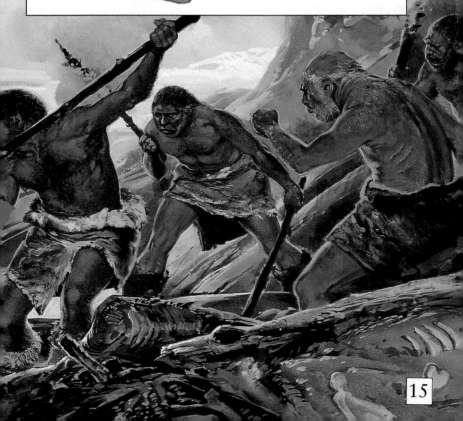

Modern people

The first modern humans were the Cro-Magnons, who began to live in Europe about 40,000 years ago. These new people stood more upright than the Neanderthals, and they had smaller faces and lighter skulls. They also made better tools, using bone, wood and stone.

KEY TO CRO-MAGNON CAMP

① Around 25,000 years ago, people in Europe hunted bison, deer, wild horses – maybe even mammoths.

② They used wooden spears, tipped with sharp flint stones.

③ Tents were made from skins stretched over wooden frames, with a fire-pit inside.

④ Animal hides were scraped, dried and cured over a fire to make clothing. The meat of the animals was roasted.

Painted rocks

Around 25,000 years ago, people all over the world began to decorate their cave walls with amazing paintings and carvings. Many of them showed the wild animals that lived at this time.

The pictures may have something to do with their religion, or with some kind of magic ceremony – we'll never know for sure !

PAINT A PEBBLE PICTURE

You will need a large, smooth pebble, a thin, black felt-tipped pen, some powder paints, a paint brush, and some polyurethane varnish.

1 Draw an animal shape on the pebble, using the black felt-tipped pen.

2 Mix some red, yellow and white powder paints with a little water, and use them to colour the animal.

3 When the paint is dry, give the pebble a coat of clear varnish.

Tools and trinkets

Luckily for us, the Cro-Magnons were untidy home-makers! They left a lot of rubbish lying around their camps, and scientists have picked up many clues about the tools they used.

They made knives and arrows from flint, and carved antlers into spear-heads. Bone was also used for lamps, hooks for catching fish, and needles for sewing hides into warm clothing.

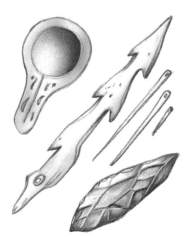

◁ (Left to right) a lamp, spearhead, needles, and an arrowhead.

▷ Finds from ancient graves show us that early people loved jewellery. They also decorated clothes with ivory, shells and bone.

A STONE AGE NECKLACE

You will need some peanuts, feathers, seeds, a needle and thread, varnish.

1 Take a long piece of thread, and sew on the nuts and seeds. Knot the thread after each piece.

2 Either push the needle through the bottom of the leaves and feathers, or tie them on tightly.

3 To make your necklace long-lasting, varnish the leaves, nuts and seeds.

Village people

About 10,000 years ago, people stopped relying on hunting for their food, and began to farm it instead. They settled in villages, and built solid houses from wood and thatched straw.

In the fields, they grew crops such as barley and wheat, and kept animals like sheep and goats. They learnt to spin and weave wool into clothes and blankets, and to make pots from clay.

THE DAILY GRIND

After the crops had been harvested, the women of the village ground the grain into flour. They did this by rubbing the seeds back and forth between a rock and a flat millstone. The grain and flour were kept in great pots, which were made from clay.

Clay and fire

People began making clay pots about 13,000 years ago. Pots were perfect for storing food and water – some of them even had tops, to keep insects and mice away.

At first, the pots were just left out in the sun to dry. But in time, people discovered that baking the clay in an oven was quicker, and made the pots much harder and stronger.

MAKE A CLAY POT

You will need some
self-hardening clay,
some paints or felt-
tips, and varnish.

1 Roll out a piece
of clay. Mark a
circle with a cup,
and cut it out to
make a base.

2 Roll some more clay
into long, thin sausages.
Coil them around the base,
to make the sides of the pot.

3 Smooth the sides, using
fingers dipped in water.

4 Leave to dry. You can
then give your pot a bright
pattern, using paints or
felt-tips. Finish with a coat
of varnish.

Giant temples

Religion was very important to early people. In many places, heavy slabs of stone called megaliths were used to build huge monuments. People visited these 'temples' to worship their gods. These may have been the Sun and the Moon, but no one knows for sure.

Stonehenge, in England, is one of the best-known monuments. It was built and rebuilt between 4,500 and 3,500 years ago.

THE MAKING OF STONEHENGE

① The biggest stones weighed about 26 tonnes, and were hauled along on log rollers.
② A hole with a sloping side was dug, and the stone was lowered into it.
③ The stone was then pulled upright with ropes, and wedged with rocks.

④ Another stone was placed alongside.
⑤ A smaller lintel stone, weighing about 7 tonnes, was levered up slowly onto a cradle of wood, row by row, until it was level with the upright stones.
⑥ Finally, the lintel stone was pushed onto the uprights.

The first miners

The Stone Age ended about 6,000 years ago, when people discovered that metal made much better points and blades for their tools and weapons. The first metal to be used was copper. Miners dug out the ore, crushed it to get at the copper, and carried it down to their furnaces to be smelted.

KEY TO MINE

① Miners bring the copper ore out of the tunnels.
② The ore is crushed.
③ Ore is washed clean.
④ Ore is smelted.

HAMILTON COLLEGE

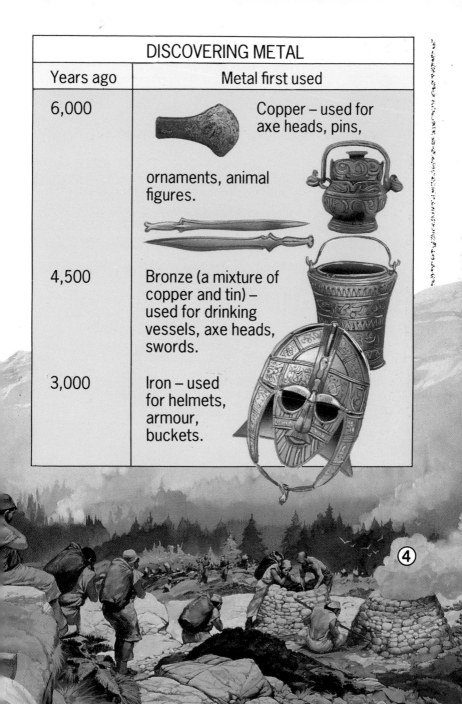

DISCOVERING METAL

Years ago	Metal first used
6,000	Copper – used for axe heads, pins, ornaments, animal figures.
4,500	Bronze (a mixture of copper and tin) – used for drinking vessels, axe heads, swords.
3,000	Iron – used for helmets, armour, buckets.

④

Glossary

ancestor – a person who is related to someone, but who lived long ago

ape – an animal like a monkey, but without a tail

cure – a way of making food keep for a long time

flint – a type of hard stone which can be chipped to make a sharp tool

hide – the skin and fur of an animal

Ice Age – a time, long ago, when most of the Earth was covered by ice and snow

lintel – a stone that is laid across two upright stones

mammoth – a type of elephant that had a hairy coat, but died out around 10,000 years ago

megalith – an enormous block of stone

monument – a building that is put up to celebrate something

ore – a type of rock that contains metal

smelt – to get the metal out of an ore by melting it

tool – an object used to help do work, such as a knife or an axe

Index